COMETS

by

HERBERT S. ZIM

illustrated by
GUSTAV SCHROTTER

William Morrow and Company

LIBRARY EDITION 1970
RESPONSIVE ENVIRONMENTS CORP.
Englewood Cliffs, N.J. 07632

The author is grateful for the aid received from those with expert competence in the field. His special thanks go to Dr. Fletcher Watson, Harvard University, Cambridge, Mass.

Printed in the United States of America.
Library of Congress Catalog Card Number: 56–8483

. . . .

SATURN

URANUS

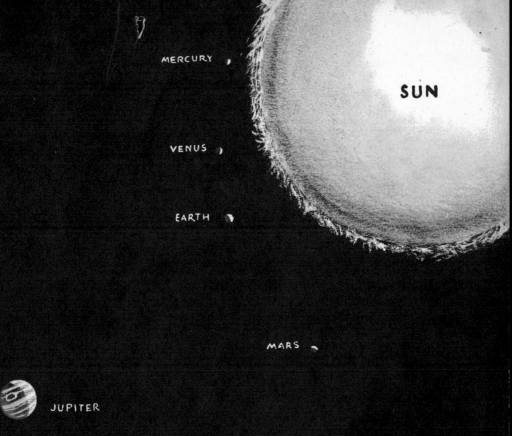

MERCURY

SUN

VENUS

EARTH

MARS

JUPITER

Around our blazing sun is a family of small heavenly bodies—small, that is, compared to the sun itself. The sun is so huge and heavy that it makes up well over 99 per cent of what we call our solar system.

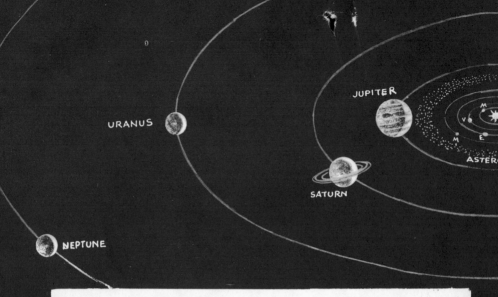

This solar family centers around the sun and includes nine planets (one of which is the earth) and some 31 moons, or satellites. It also includes over a thousand asteroids. These are tiny planets which circle the sun, mostly between the paths of Mars and Jupiter. The smallest asteroids are no larger than a mountain; the largest is 480 miles in diameter.

JUPITER WITH ITS
4 LARGEST MOONS

SATURN WITH SOME
OF ITS 9 MOONS

Finally, the solar family includes many comets and even more meteors. Comets and meteors definitely belong to the solar system, although the sun's hold on some is barely enough to keep them in the solar family. The more astronomers study comets and meteors, the more they feel that they are related to each other. Although comets are not important in the tremendous universe or even within our small solar family, they are among the most curious of all the heavenly bodies.

AHNIGHITO METEORITE
BROUGHT FROM GREENLAND
BY ADMIRAL PEARY
WEIGHT 36½ TONS

STONY METEORITE
FELL IN NORTH CAROLINA
ON APRIL 21, 1913

People knew something about the sun thousands of years ago. They named the large, bright planets, which slowly wandered across the night sky. They learned, too, that the sun, moon, and planets travel regular paths, which go through a circular band of twelve constellations called the zodiac. Centuries ago, people learned to map the paths of the sun and the planets and to predict their motion. But comets and meteors were another matter.

THE SUN SEEMS TO MOVE PAST THE
CONSTELLATIONS OF THE ZODIAC

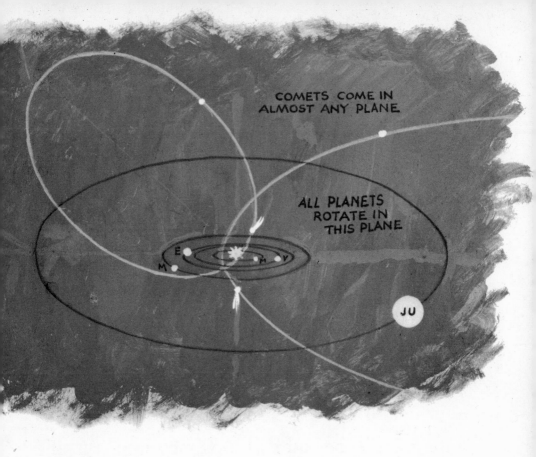

COMETS COME IN
ALMOST ANY PLANE.

ALL PLANETS
ROTATE IN
THIS PLANE

JU

Comets may appear in almost any part of the sky, not just in the zodiac, where the planets are seen. In early times no one could predict their coming. They moved slowly across the sky in flaming streaks of light that terrified everyone. Even today some people are afraid of comets. There is still much to be learned about these mysterious members of the solar family, but no one should fear them.

People often think of comets as huge blazing stars with long tails streaming behind them. Yet most comets have little or no tail, and nearly all of them are invisible except through a telescope. A few comets are big and spread across a larger part of the sky than any other heavenly body we know of. But these big comets are not what they appear to be. They weigh very little. They are mainly empty space. The truth is, as one great astronomer put it, "A comet is the nearest thing to nothing that anything can be and still be something." But if a comet is practically nothing, it is certainly a most unusual piece of nothing.

COMET OF 1456 PASSING THE CONSTELLATIONS
OF LEO AND CANCER

FROM AN OLD PRINT

In olden days the only comets known were the large, brilliant ones that could be seen with the naked eye. They appeared without warning, and they looked so big and bright that people thought they were very close to the earth. Our great-great-grandparents believed that comets were messengers of evil, bringing disease, war, and destruction. When one appeared, people thronged to churches to pray. Merchants did a thriving business selling charms to protect the wearer from the comet.

The ancient Chinese, who were much interested in astronomy, were not worried about comets. They pictured comets in their ancient records and wrote of them as messengers going from one part of the heavens to another. To the Chinese, the comet's long tail was a broom that swept the skies clean.

ANCIENT CHINESE OBSERVATORY
WHERE POSITIONS OF
STARS AND COMETS
WERE RECORDED

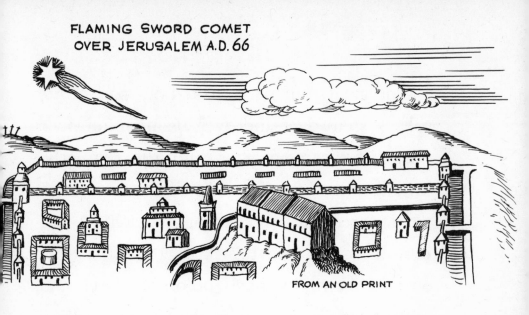

FROM AN OLD PRINT

The great comets were so fearsome and so spectacular that people kept records of their coming long before the days of books and printing. Some of the earliest records, however, are not very clear. The great Jewish writer Josephus spoke of the "sword," which stood over Jerusalem just before it fell to the Romans in the year 70 A.D. The sword was probably a great comet seen over Jerusalem in the year 66 A.D. Since its nearly straight tail pointed toward the horizon, it probably did look something like a sword. Chinese records of comets date as far back as 600 B.C.

One great comet has visited our part of the solar system over and over again, about once every 75 years. Since it returns regularly, scholars think they can identify this comet in written records back through each 75-year period to the year 467 B.C. From that time on, the accounts have become clearer and more scientific each time the brilliant comet has returned.

When this great comet appeared in the year 1066, King Harold, new on the English throne, was sorely troubled by it. William the

COMET OF 1066
SHOWN IN
BAYEUX
TAPESTRY

Conqueror was preparing a fleet of ships to attack England from Normandy. England was soon conquered by the Normans and King Harold was killed. The famous Bayeux tapestry, woven to record the great events of that time, shows the comet clearly.

In 1577 another great comet appeared; this time the astronomer Tycho Brahe discovered the first clue about the real nature of comets. This man, who was the first modern scientific astronomer, watched the comet from his own observatory at the edge of the Baltic Sea. Then, after a hurried voyage, he observed it again from the city of Prague.

SERVATORY OF TYCHO BRAHE
ILT FOR HIM BY THE KING OF
DENMARK IN 1576

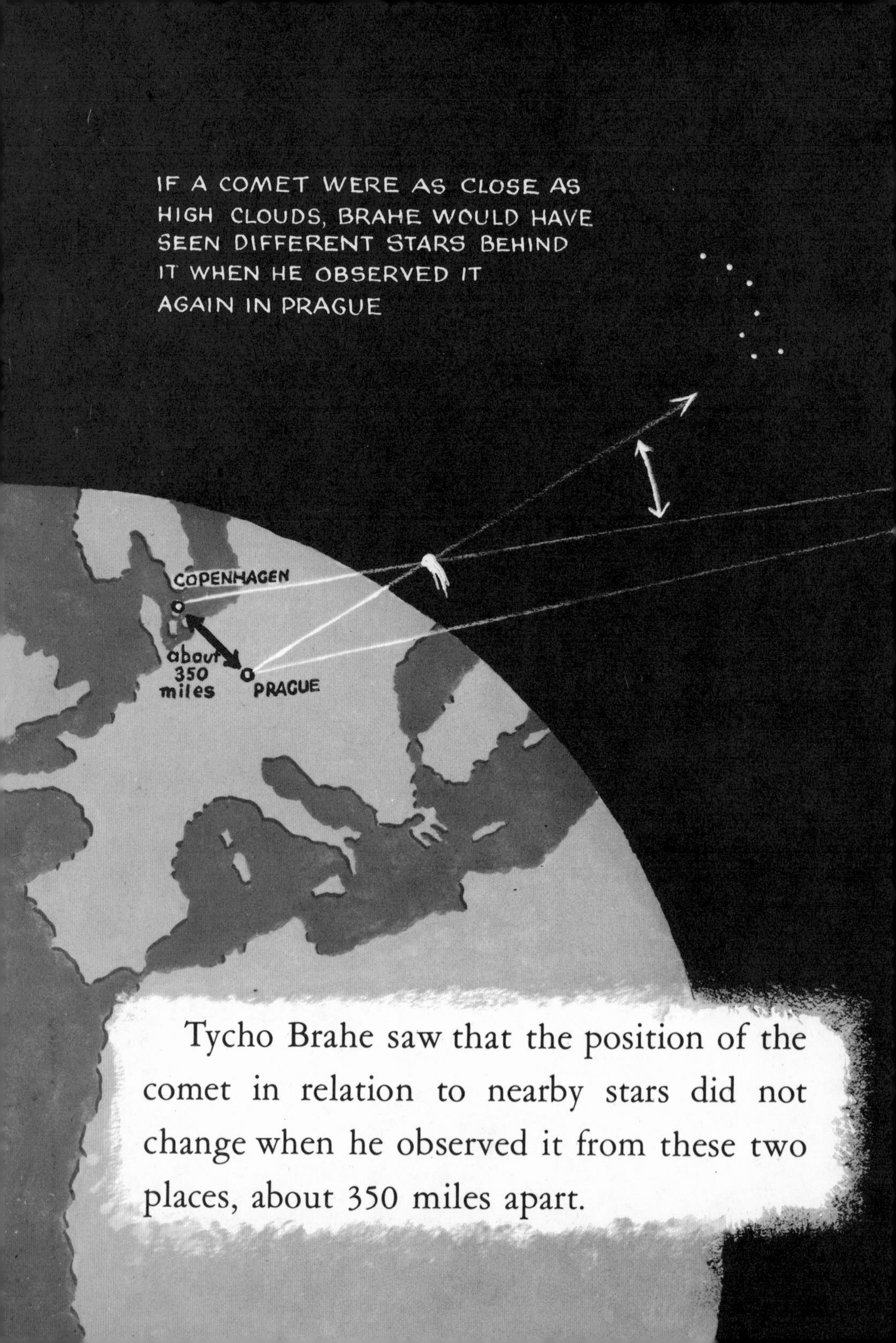

IF A COMET WERE AS CLOSE AS
HIGH CLOUDS, BRAHE WOULD HAVE
SEEN DIFFERENT STARS BEHIND
IT WHEN HE OBSERVED IT
AGAIN IN PRAGUE

COPENHAGEN

about
350
miles   PRAGUE

Tycho Brahe saw that the position of the
comet in relation to nearby stars did not
change when he observed it from these two
places, about 350 miles apart.

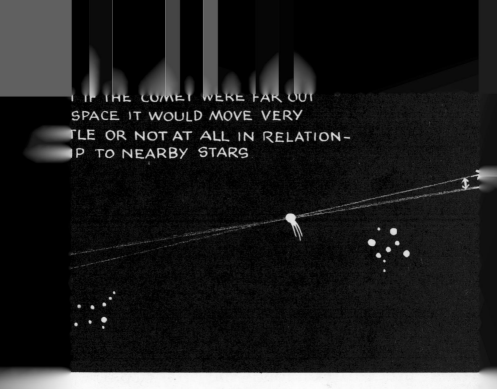

IF THE COMET WERE FAR OUT
SPACE IT WOULD MOVE VERY
TLE OR NOT AT ALL IN RELATION-
P TO NEARBY STARS

By the use of simple mathematics, Tycho Brahe figured out that the comet was at least several times as far away as the moon. This one fact freed countless people from fear, for since everyone believed that the large comets were very close to the earth, they thought them dangerous, bringing disease and pestilence. Brahe proved that a comet was a normal part of the heavens: something that could be studied, rather than an omen to be feared.

Little more than a century later, an Englishman named Edmund Halley took another great step forward in the study of comets. He was a friend of Sir Isaac Newton, and published Newton's famous book at his own expense. Newton's ideas about gravity, speed, and motion made it possible for Halley to unravel the comet's mystery. 51

Halley had seen the great comet of 1682 and had read about the bright comets which had appeared in 1531 and 1607. He studied charts showing their position, and from them he figured out their paths or orbits.

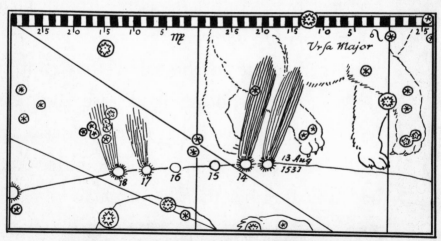

CHART USED BY HALLEY TO HELP CHART
THE ORBIT OF THE COMET OF 1531

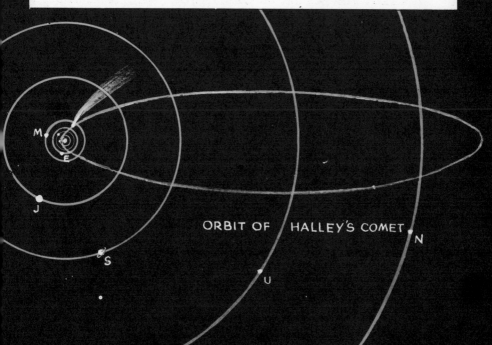

HALLEY'S COMET
MAY 6, 1910

When he had finished, Halley was certain that the three comets were really one, which traveled on a long elliptical path that extended far out from the sun past all the planets known at that time. Knowing the size of the orbit and the comet's speed, Halley predicted that this comet would return again in 1758.

ORBIT OF HALLEY'S COMET

Halley died in 1742, and many people for-
got his prediction. But on Christmas day of
1758 an amateur astronomer located the comet
again. At first its light was very faint, but as it
came closer to the sun and the earth, it grew
brighter. All through the spring of 1759
nothing rivaled it in the sky. It has been
known as Halley's comet ever since. 2/7

The word *comet* comes from a Greek word

PHOTOS OF HALLEY'S COMET SOON AFTER ITS
DISCOVERY ON ITS LAST RETURN IN 1909.
IT WAS VISIBLE FROM SEPT. 1909 TILL MAY 1911

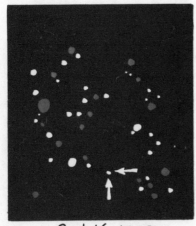 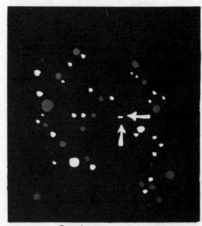

Sept. 16, 1909   Sept. 24, 1909

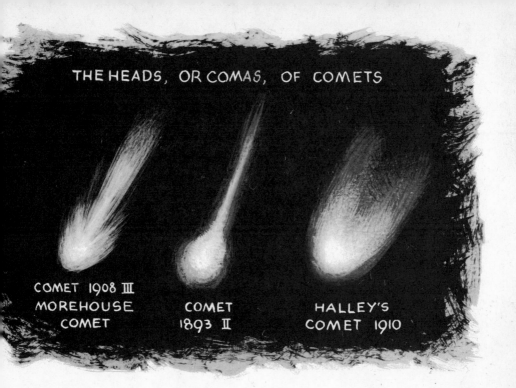

THE HEADS, OR COMAS, OF COMETS

COMET 1908 III
MOREHOUSE
COMET

COMET
1893 II

HALLEY'S
COMET 1910

meaning hair, which describes the comet's tail. But scientists use the name *coma* for the misty disk which makes up the comet's head. This coma makes comets look quite different from the stars, which appear to us as clear, sharp points of light. Sometimes this fuzzy coma and its special orbit are all that mark a comet, for most of the known comets seem to consist of a coma and little more.

As comets come closer to the sun, a brighter spot of light called the nucleus may be seen near the center of the coma. If a comet gets still closer to the sun, a tail may begin to form. The tail grows longer as the comet gets closer, and shorter as it moves away, until it finally disappears. No approaching comet with a tail has been seen farther away than the planet Mars, or about 150 million miles.

NUCLEUS IN HEAD
OF HALLEY'S COMET
MAY 5, 1910

In ancient days, comets were observed with the unaided eye. There was no other way. After the telescope was invented, in the early 1600's, comets could be seen in greater detail and fainter comets were discovered. Today nearly all the study of comets is done through telescopes. Instead of watching the comet directly, an astronomer usually takes telescopic photographs. These give him a permanent record to study and compare with other pictures.

GALILEO'S
TELESCOPES
1609
The top one
magnified
32 times

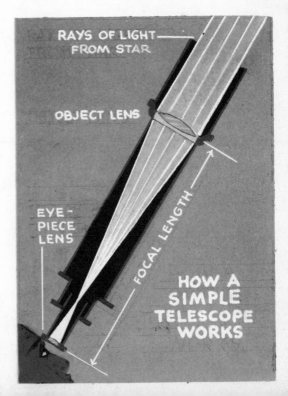

RAYS OF LIGHT FROM STAR

OBJECT LENS

EYE-PIECE LENS

FOCAL LENGTH

HOW A SIMPLE TELESCOPE WORKS

Light from a comet can be directed through the telescope into other devices. The spectroscope, which splits and spreads a beam of light according to its color, is the most important of them. When a band of light is thus spread out, dark or bright lines may appear across it. These lines tell what chemicals are present in the comet or the star.

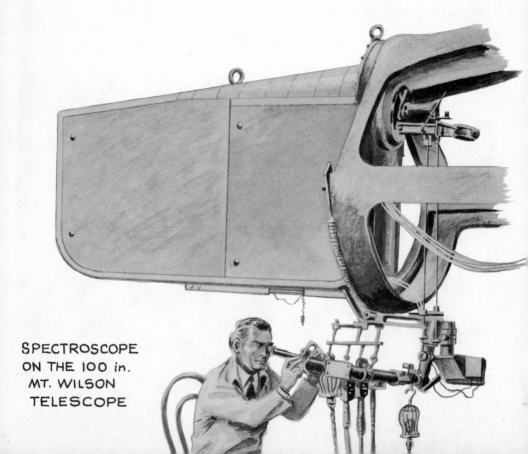

SPECTROSCOPE
ON THE 100 in.
MT. WILSON
TELESCOPE

Comets can be measured and to some extent weighed. The weight of comets is figured out in two ways: by the effect they have on the planets they pass, and by the effect that these heavenly bodies have on the comets. Everything that has weight has a pull, which we call gravity. The heavier the star or planet, the greater its pull. A very heavy comet would have a strong pull and might affect the orbit of a moon or planet as it came close.

By charting the position of a comet against the stars seen behind it, astronomers can plot its path and reckon its speed. The path of a comet can be charted roughly as soon as its position can be checked three different times. Only three positions are needed to plot a curve.

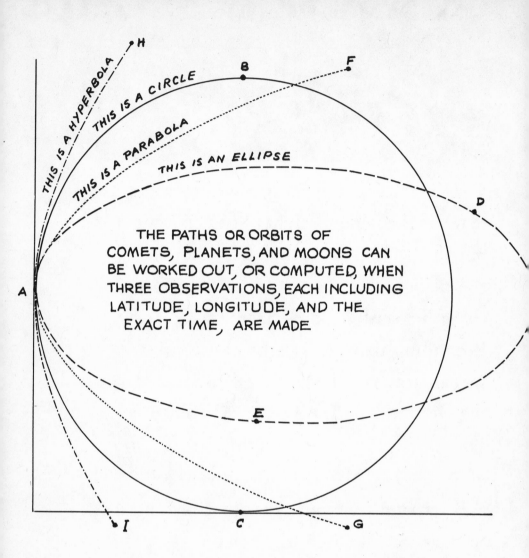

THIS IS A HYPERBOLA

THIS IS A CIRCLE

THIS IS A PARABOLA

THIS IS AN ELLIPSE

THE PATHS OR ORBITS OF
COMETS, PLANETS, AND MOONS CAN
BE WORKED OUT, OR COMPUTED, WHEN
THREE OBSERVATIONS, EACH INCLUDING
LATITUDE, LONGITUDE, AND THE
EXACT TIME, ARE MADE.

Since all comets travel on curved paths,
their orbits can be roughly mapped from three
observations. If more are taken, the comet's
path can be charted very accurately.

As a result of these studies, astronomers now know that the head of a comet is nothing more than a huge cloud of gas surrounding some solid material from which the gases

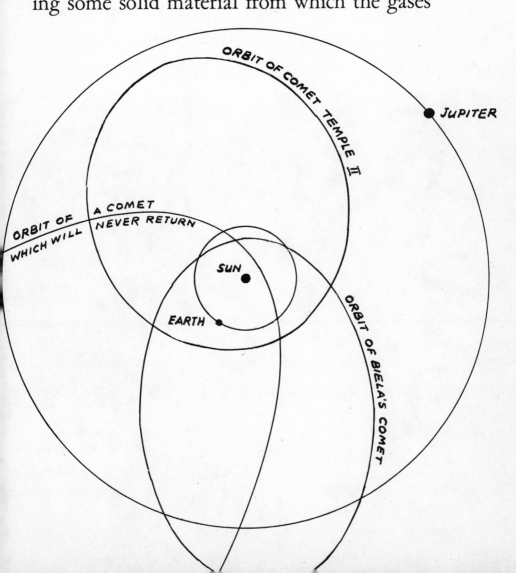

come. Most of what we see is very thin gas, so there is very little to a comet's head. The head may be very large; often it is as big as the earth or even the giant planet Jupiter. The heads of a few comets are even larger than the sun. Their heads, however, weigh very little; they are practically nothing.

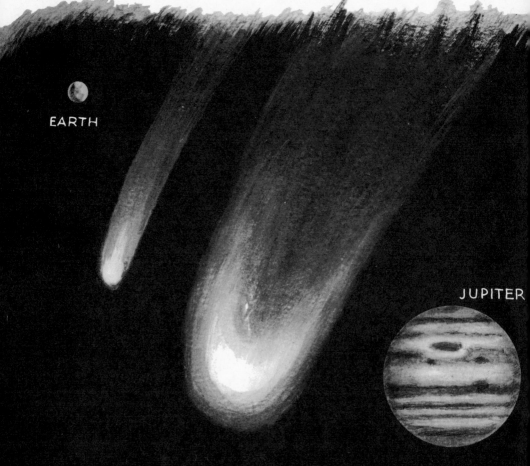

EARTH

JUPITER

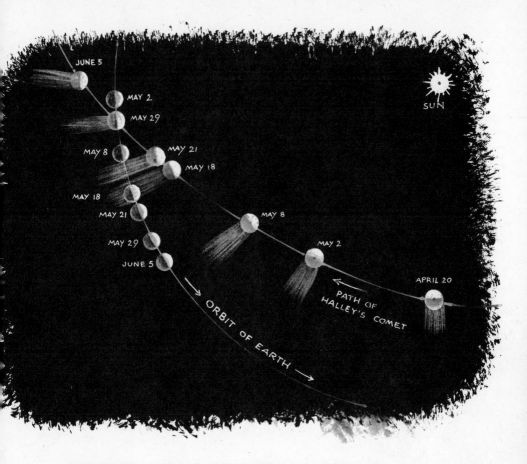

THE EARTH ALSO PASSED VERY CLOSE TO
HALLEY'S COMET IN 1910. THE COMET
HAD NO EFFECT IN CHANGING THE
ORBIT OF THE EARTH

One comet passed so close to the earth in
1770 that the small gravitational pull of the
earth definitely changed the comet's orbit. Yet
the comet had no effect on the earth. This

meant that the comet weighed very little compared to the earth. Further evidence comes
from studying the relatively large effect Jupiter and the sun have on passing comets. All
these findings prove that the head of a comet
is very light. The largest one probably weighs
only one millionth of the earth's weight.

Now you can see what an astronomer means

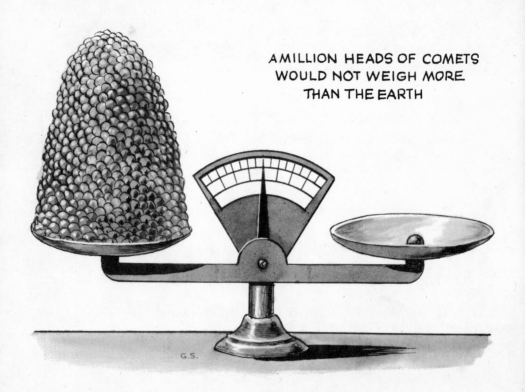

AMILLION HEADS OF COMETS
WOULD NOT WEIGH MORE
THAN THE EARTH

when he says that a comet is practically nothing. A millionth of the weight of the earth,
though very little, amounts to about a million
million tons. This is far greater than the
weight of all the buildings, houses, monu-
ments, machines, and products that man has
ever made. Yet when you consider the heavens,
with millions upon millions of stars which
average as big or bigger than our own sun, a
comet weighing only a million million tons
seems as small as a grain of dust.

The nucleus in the head of a comet is a bright spot, but it does not seem to get larger when viewed through a telescope. Jets of bright gas sometimes shoot out from the nucleus when the comet is near the sun. But no one is sure what the nucleus is. One astronomer believes it to be a spongy mass of frozen gases—colder than any snow on earth. Dust and small stones may be mixed with this "snow" made of carbon dioxide and other gases.

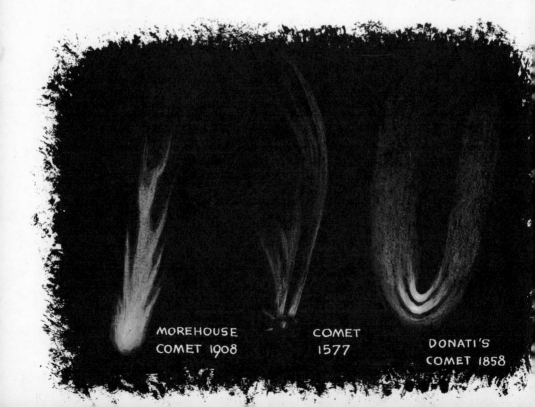

MOREHOUSE COMET 1908

COMET 1577

DONATI'S COMET 1858

HOW THE TAIL OF A COMET FORMS
CUNNINGHAM'S COMET 1940

When a comet approaching the sun gets inside the orbit of Mars, a tail may begin to form right out of the head. At first it is short, making the comet look like a polliwog. Then the material streams farther and farther out, always away from the sun. By the time the comet has come within the earth's orbit, the tail may be several million miles long. Growing rapidly, the longest tail may finally extend a hundred million miles or even more.

MILLION MILE RULER

TAILS OF COMETS GROW FROM 1 MILLION TO 100 MILLION MILES LONG

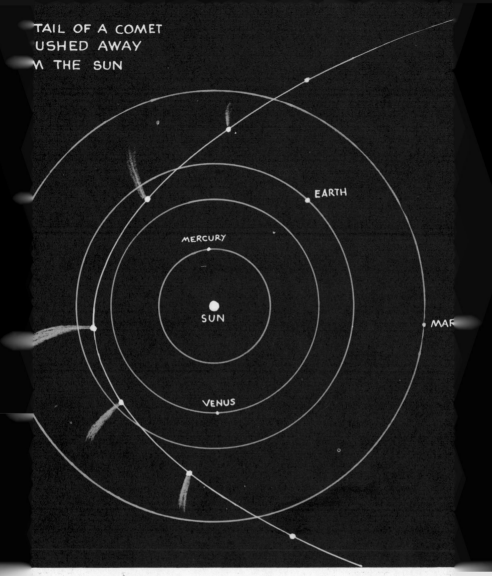

The tail may form a straight line or a curve, depending on the angle at which we see the comet. But it always points away from the sun. It does not necessarily show the direction that the comet is traveling. As a comet approaches the sun, the tail will probably be behind the comet. Near the sun it swings off at an angle, and when the comet leaves the sun it will stream ahead.

The material that makes up the tail of the comet comes from the solid material in the nucleus. As the nucleus is heated by sunlight, bits of dust and gas come loose and spread outward. The pressure of the sun's light helps to force these particles back, forming the tail.

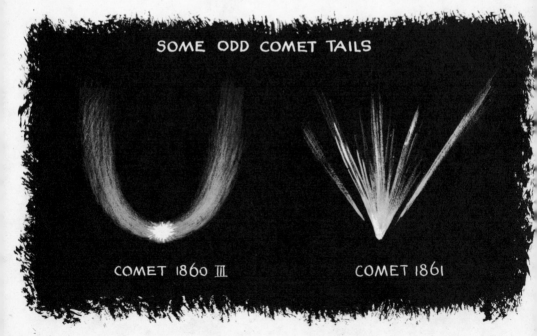

SOME ODD COMET TAILS

COMET 1860 III   COMET 1861

The idea that light has push, or pressure, sounds strange. If you hold your hand near an electric light or in the sunlight, you cannot feel light pressing on it. Nevertheless, light does have pressure. It is only noticeable when the light becomes extremely strong, as it is near the sun, and it affects only very small particles, like molecules of gas or the very finest particles of dust. This pressure of light is called radiation pressure. The closer a comet gets to the sun, the greater the effect of radiation pressure upon it.

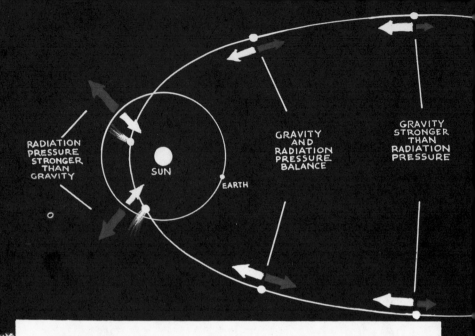

RADIATION
PRESSURE
STRONGER
THAN
GRAVITY

SUN

EARTH

GRAVITY
AND
RADIATION
PRESSURE
BALANCE

GRAVITY
STRONGER
THAN
RADIATION
PRESSURE

When a comet is far away from the sun, all the forces acting on it, including the sun's gravity, are very weak. But as it gets closer to the sun, both gravity and radiation pressure increase, and balance one another. Other forces, perhaps electrical, enter the picture. Near the sun these forces may be a hundred times as great as the pull of the sun's gravity. At this point heat releases gases and dust from the comet's head. These are pushed away from the sun instead of being pulled toward it.

The tail of a comet contains even less matter than the head. Some large scientific laboratories have wonderful devices for pumping all the air out of a container until only a few molecules are left. This is as near as we can get to a perfect vacuum. The tail of a comet has about as little material in it as the best vacuum we

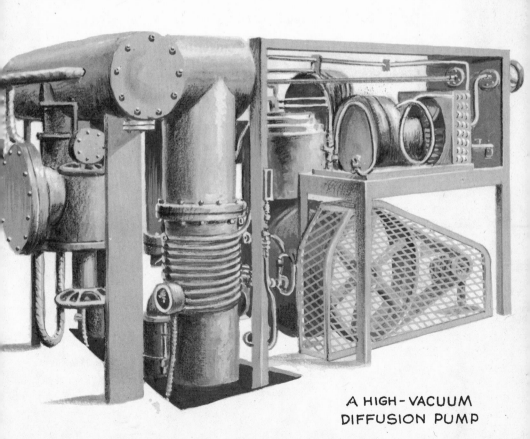

A HIGH-VACUUM
DIFFUSION PUMP

can make. If the air in the room where you are sitting could be spread out to cover a space about the size of the earth, it would contain about as many molecules as the tail of a comet. The tail is so thin that the earth could pass through it with no effect worth mentioning. In 1910 the earth did brush the tail of Halley's comet, and a careful check showed that its pull did not affect the earth in any way.

MOON

EARTH

ON MAY 18, 1916
THE EARTH
BRUSHED THE
TAIL OF
HALLEY'S COMET
(see chart page 27)

DONATI'S COMET 1858 WITH STARS
SEEN UNDIMMED THROUGH THE TAIL

Another proof that a comet is made of practically nothing is that stars can be seen behind
it just as clearly as though it were not there at
all. When Halley's comet crossed the earth's
orbit in 1910, it passed between the earth and
the sun. If the head of the comet were solid,
it would have appeared dark against the sun,

as the planets Venus and Mercury do when they pass between the earth and the sun. But no trace of a shadow of the comet was seen. Another comet came so close to the earth in 1927 that it was possible to take very exact measurements of its head. These measurements showed that it did not contain any solid bodies larger than about a mile in diameter.

VENUS

COMETS
DO NOT CAST
A SHADOW ON
THE SUN AS DO
PLANETS WHEN
THEY PASS
BETWEEN THE SUN
AND THE EARTH

TRANSIT OF VENUS

Since there is so little matter in a comet, it is natural to wonder why it shines. Part of the light from a comet is sunlight reflected from the bits of material in it. Most of the reflected light seems to come from the nucleus, which glows brighter as the comet gets closer to the sun. The earth, the moon, and other planets also shine by reflected light.

A comet is also exposed to the sun's strong ultraviolet light. This light excites the gases in a comet and makes them glow like the light from a fluorescent lamp. In effect, the short waves of invisible ultraviolet light from the sun are changed into longer, visible rays. Much of the light from the comet and all of the light from the tail forms in this way.

The bits of material torn away from the head of a comet to form the tail are lost forever, so the comet gradually gets smaller and smaller. Sometimes a small comet burns itself out in a single trip around the sun. Even large comets, which return time and time again, may be getting fainter because they lose more material each time they swing around the sun. The material lost by comets drifts away into outer space.

The spectroscope helps scientists decide what comets are made of, and it also indicates conditions within the head of the comet. It proves, for example, that comets are not very hot in comparison to stars, because their chemical elements are combined into mole-

BANDED SPECTRUM OF CYANOGEN GAS (CN)
THIS GAS IS FOUND IN COMETS

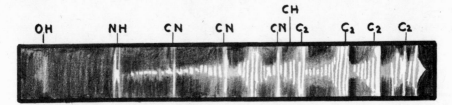

**SPECTRUM OF CUNNINGHAM COMET 1940
WITH MOLECULES IDENTIFIED**

cules, somewhat as they are on earth. Molecules do not form on very hot stars.

The elements in the heads of comets include carbon, hydrogen, nitrogen, and oxygen. All of these are found in our air. Some of these elements are combined into molecules: carbon with oxygen, carbon with hydrogen, carbon with nitrogen, and nitrogen with hydrogen.

ELEMENTS AND MOLECULES FOUND IN COMETS
WITH THEIR CHEMICAL ABBREVIATIONS

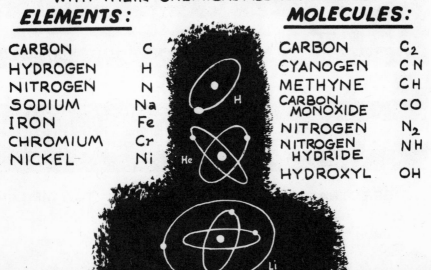

ELEMENTS:

CARBON	C
HYDROGEN	H
NITROGEN	N
SODIUM	Na
IRON	Fe
CHROMIUM	Cr
NICKEL	Ni

MOLECULES:

CARBON	C_2
CYANOGEN	CN
METHYNE	CH
CARBON MONOXIDE	CO
NITROGEN	N_2
NITROGEN HYDRIDE	NH
HYDROXYL	OH

As a comet gets closer to the sun, however, it does get hotter and hotter. It may even get hot enough to change metals into glowing vapors. The telltale light from these vapors has been picked up by spectroscopes. They show that certain metals—sodium, iron, and possibly nickel and chromium may be found in comets. Because the light from comets is not completely explained, other elements and molecules may be discovered in the future, but it is far more difficult to study light from comets than from the sun or bright stars.

SPECTRAL LINES OF THE GASES OF TWO METALS

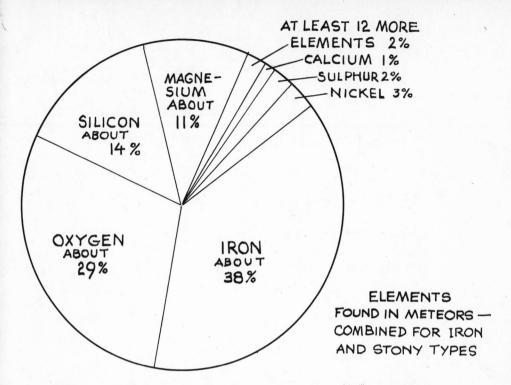

AT LEAST 12 MORE ELEMENTS 2%
CALCIUM 1%
SULPHUR 2%
NICKEL 3%

MAGNE-SIUM ABOUT 11%

SILICON ABOUT 14%

OXYGEN ABOUT 29%

IRON ABOUT 38%

ELEMENTS FOUND IN METEORS — COMBINED FOR IRON AND STONY TYPES

A number of comets are known to be associated with meteors, or falling stars. The chemicals in meteors that have struck the earth have been studied and are well known. They may give a clue to the chemicals in comets. Some meteorites are mainly iron; others are stony. No chemicals have been found in any of them that have not already been found on the earth. This will probably be true of comets, also.

The paths of some comets have been mapped carefully, and astronomers can predict when they will appear again. This is especially true of the small minor comets. Three groups of them move around their orbits in periods of five to twelve years, thirteen to eighteen years, and about twenty-eight years. Halley's is the

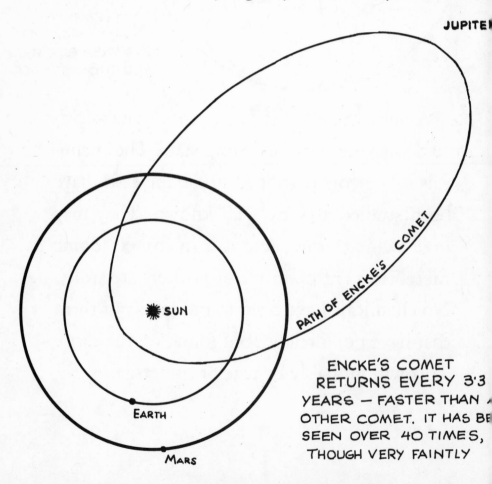

JUPITER

PATH OF ENCKE'S COMET

☀ SUN

EARTH

MARS

ENCKE'S COMET RETURNS EVERY 3·3 YEARS — FASTER THAN OTHER COMET. IT HAS BE SEEN OVER 40 TIMES, THOUGH VERY FAINTLY

TIME TABLE FOR HALLEY'S COMET

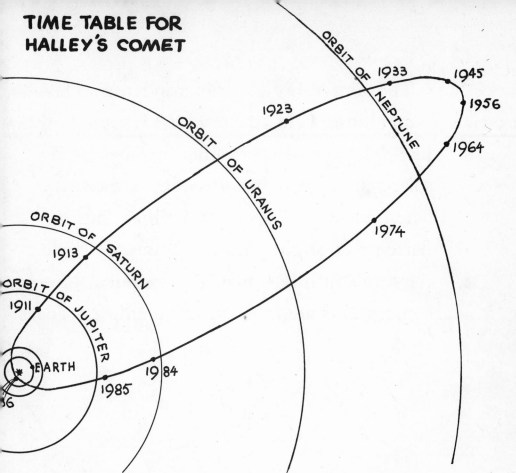

only major comet with a well-mapped orbit. It reached its farthest distance from the sun in 1947, and now it has started back toward the earth and sun again. It is due back in 1986, so any young person reading this book will have a good chance of seeing this large and famous comet himself.

The orbit of Halley's comet and many others is an ellipse, a closed curve that is something like a flattened circle. Other members of the solar system move in paths of the same shape The orbit of the earth is an ellipse, but it is flattened so slightly that it is almost a circle; the orbits of others planets are similar. Most comet orbits are more flattened ellipses. The

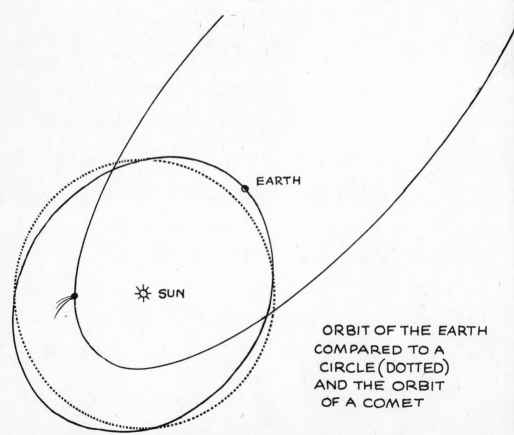

EARTH

☼ SUN

ORBIT OF THE EARTH
COMPARED TO A
CIRCLE (DOTTED)
AND THE ORBIT
OF A COMET

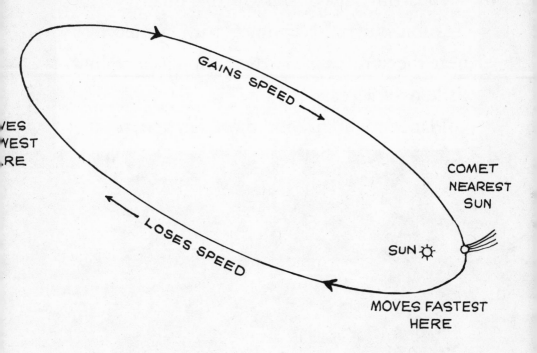

GAINS SPEED →

VES
VEST
RE

COMET
NEAREST
SUN

LOSES SPEED

SUN ☼

MOVES FASTEST
HERE

orbit of Halley's comet extends past the orbit
of Neptune.

The speed of a comet on an elliptical orbit
varies with its position. The nearer it is to
the sun, the faster it moves. If its orbit was
a circle, a comet's speed would be the same
in any position. The flatter the ellipse, the
greater the changes in speed. Halley's comet

spends thirty-two years in the small part of its orbit outside Neptune's path. When it is near the sun it covers the same distance in a little over a year.

Planets, which have more circular orbits,

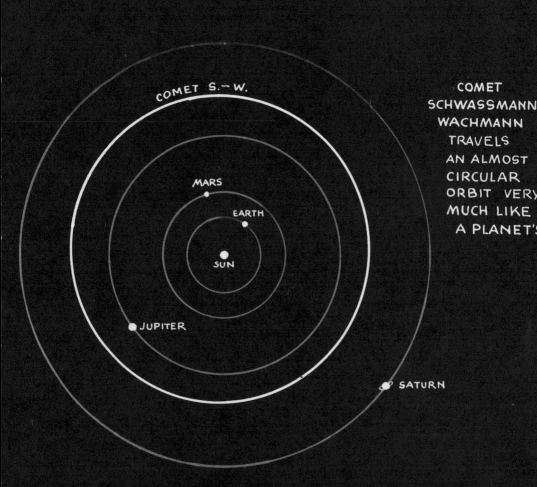

COMET S.—W.

COMET
SCHWASSMANN
WACHMANN
TRAVELS
AN ALMOST
CIRCULAR
ORBIT VERY
MUCH LIKE
A PLANET'S

MARS

EARTH

SUN

JUPITER

SATURN

travel at more regular speeds. One comet with a planetlike orbit circles the sun in seventeen years. If a planet came so close that its pull speeded up or slowed down this comet, its orbit would also change. If it gained enough speed, its new orbit might take the comet completely out of the solar system.

As soon as a new comet is discovered, it is officially reported by coded telegram to the Harvard Observatory in this country or to the Copenhagen Observatory in Europe. The message gives the comet's position, and at once astronomers begin to check its orbit. Many comets have fairly small elliptical orbits, which are easily checked. There is no doubt that they belong to the solar system. The evidence indicates, although it does not prove, that all the others do too.

The orbits of over a third of the comets seem to be open curves, but more likely they are closed curves so large that scientists, studying only a very small part of the orbit, cannot be sure. If an elliptical orbit is very large it may take a comet hundreds, thousands, or even millions of years to return to the vicinity of the sun. Many orbits of this size are known.

The orbits of comets may change too. Comets are attracted by planets, especially by Jupiter. If one comes close, the pull of Jupiter changes its orbit somewhat. The next time the comet passes Jupiter, its orbit changes still more. Usually the new orbit is smaller than the original orbit. When a comet passes near Jupiter fairly often, it is counted as a member of Jupiter's family of comets.

A CURVE THIS LARGE MIGHT BE PART OF AN OPEN CURVE OR OF A LARGE ELLIPSE. ONLY FURTHER STUDY OF MORE OF THE CURVE WILL GIVE THE ANSWER

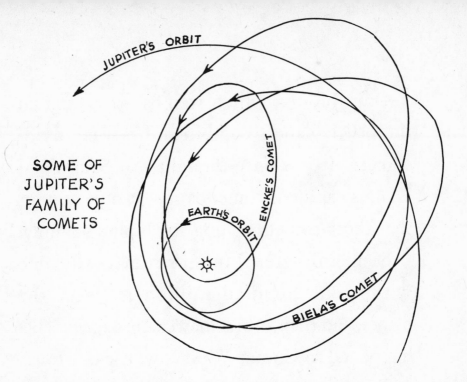

SOME OF
JUPITER'S
FAMILY OF
COMETS

JUPITER'S ORBIT

ENCKE'S COMET

EARTH'S ORBIT

BIELA'S COMET

The shape of the new orbit depends on the speed of the captured comet, on its original path, and on its distance from Jupiter. About two dozen of the comets that Jupiter has captured have been observed at least twice in their new orbits. Another two dozen or so also belong to Jupiter's family, but it is hard to be sure, because these comets are small and appear as only faint telescopic objects. All take from five to twelve years to revolve around the sun.

Only Jupiter, which weighs more than all the other planets combined, has a family of comets. It was once thought that Saturn and Uranus captured comets also. It now appears that these comets belong to Jupiter's family.

Sooner or later, Jupiter's comets all come within one hundred million miles of the planet, and their orbits may change again. This happened to Comet Wolf I, whose orbit was pulled from a larger to a smaller one. Forty-seven years later, as it passed Jupiter again, it was pulled back to the more distant path.

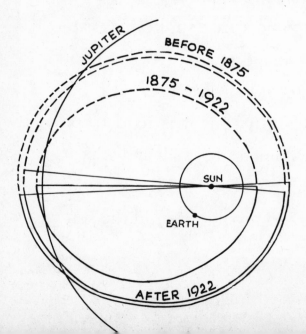

COMET WOLF I
HAS AN ORBIT
WHICH HAS BEEN
CHANGED TWICE
BY THE PULL
OF JUPITER

NEW HYPERBOLIC ORBIT

FORMER ELLIPTICAL ORBIT

ORBIT OF JUPITER

JUPITER'S PULL
CHANGING A
COMET'S ORBIT
MAY SEND IT
OUT OF THE
SOLAR SYSTEM

Jupiter's pull can also throw a comet into an open-curved, or hyperbolic orbit. This happens when a comet passes Jupiter at just the right angle for the gravitational pull of the giant planet to increase the comet's speed. If, at Jupiter's distance from the sun, this speed increases to over twelve miles a second, the comet moves into an open-curved orbit which will rapidly take it out of the solar system.

Very little is known about how comets began. Perhaps they were not a part of the original solar system. Our sun, with all its family, rushes through space at the rate of twelve miles per second. Our whole star system, or galaxy, revolves much faster. Hence, the sun may have captured a great family of comets.

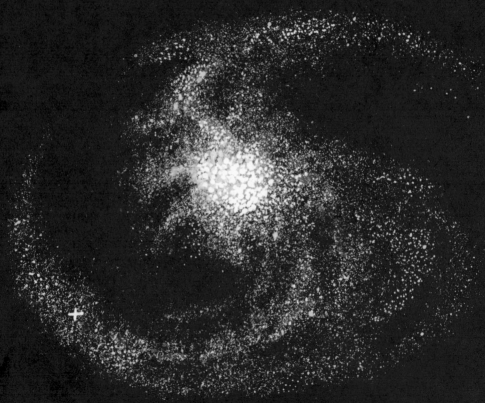

✛ THE SUN IS PART OF A GALAXY CONTAINING ABOUT 100,000,000,000 STARS. IT REVOLVES IN THE GALAXY AT A SPEED OF 120 MILES A SECOND

Some people think that comets have always been a part of the solar system. Perhaps they are part of the material left over when the sun, planets, moons, and asteroids were formed. There are a number of ideas as to how the solar system began. One is that it developed from a great dust cloud in space; another is that the planets were formed in a lens-shaped disk of gas surrounding the sun.

Until astronomers are more sure about the

beginning of the solar system, they can only guess about the origin of comets. The orbits of the planets are nearly all on the same level, or plane, and they all travel in the same direction. This is not true of comets, whose orbits are tilted at all angles. This makes it hard to explain the origin of comets and their place in the solar system.

Astronomers know much more about how comets end than how they begin. These loose clouds of dust and gas are greatly affected by the pull of gravity. Some comets react violently when they pass close to the sun. The great comet of 1882 passed within a half million miles of the sun at a speed of over a million miles an hour. Soon its nucleus split into four parts. But we shall not know whether the comet continued to split till it returns in about five to eight hundred years.

Biela's comet, which appeared late in 1845, had split in two since its last appearance six and a half years before. The new twin comets traveled close together. First one shone brighter, then the other. When these comets returned in 1852, one of the pair was very dim.

BIELA'S COMET
SPLIT ON ITS
RETURN IN 1845

The comet was never seen again. In 1872, when it was due to pass the earth, a great shower of meteors appeared instead. A hundred meteors a minute flashed through the sky. Later the meteor shower disappeared too.

GREAT LEONID SHOW

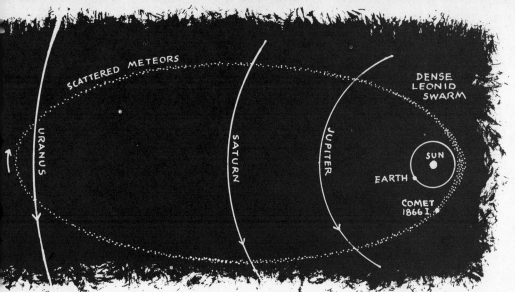

There seems to be a relation between a number of other comets and showers of meteors. As time goes on there is more and more reason to believe that the study of each will help in understanding the other.

SOME COMETS — — — AND THE METEOR SHOWERS WHICH HAVE SIMILAR ORBITS

SOME COMETS		AND THE METEOR SHOWERS WHICH HAVE SIMILAR ORBITS		Date best seen
COMET	1862 III	—	PERSEIDS	best seen AUG. 11
COMET	1861 I	—	LYRIDS	— " — APR. 21
COMET	1866 I	—	LEONIDS	— " — NOV. 15
COMET	1852 III	—	ANDROMEDES	— " — NOV. 27
COMET	1933 III	—	DRACONIDS	— " — OCT. 9
HALLEY'S COMET		—	ORIONIDS	— " — OCT. 21

The brightness of stars, planets, and comets is measured in magnitudes. First-magnitude stars are the brightest. Those of the sixth magnitude are barely seen. Before the invention of the telescope, a comet had to be brighter than sixth magnitude to be discovered. Most were of the third or fourth magnitude when they were first seen. As telescopes were improved, dimmer comets were found. Now, using a camera with a telescope, comets as faint as fifteenth or sixteenth magnitude are detected.

As a result, hundreds of comets have been discovered recently, and there are probably thousands more. One astronomer estimates that there may be a hundred thousand of them. But many might not come close enough to the earth to be seen or photographed through a telescope.

Many of the comets discovered today are found by amateur astronomers who watch the heavens carefully. From night to night they note any heavenly body which changes its position even slightly in relationship to nearby stars. Either a comet or an asteroid would do this. Larger observatories photograph portions of the skies at regular intervals, which is a better check. A few comets are discovered each year, sometimes as many as a dozen.

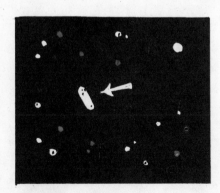 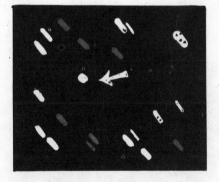

IF A TELESCOPE FOLLOWS **STARS** EXACTLY, A COMET WILL PHOTOGRAPH AS A STREAK BECAUSE OF ITS MOVEMENT

IF A TELESCOPE FOLLOWS A **COMET** EXACTLY, STARS WILL PHOTOGRAPH AS STREAKS BECAUSE THE EARTH IS TURNING

The study of the sky in general, and comets in particular, is so interesting that more and more people are attracted to it. Some day, in addition to reading about comets, you may be looking for them <u>with</u> your own telescope. Perhaps you will even discover one yourself.